ANIMALS GROWING UP™

HOW WHALES GROW UP

Lisa Idzikowski

E **Enslow Publishing**
101 W. 23rd Street
Suite 240
New York, NY 10011
USA

enslow.com

WORDS TO KNOW

baleen The comblike parts some whales have in their mouths instead of teeth.

calf A baby whale.

cow A mother whale.

krill Small shrimplike animals.

mammal An animal that has a backbone and hair; females usually give birth to live babies and produce milk to feed their young.

migrate To swim to different areas of the ocean.

predator An animal that kills and eats other animals to live.

species A group of living things that are alike and have the same scientific name.

CONTENTS

BABY WHALES

Baby whales, or calves, are huge! At birth, a blue whale calf can be as long as half a school bus. It can grow to be more than 100 feet (30 meters) long and up to 40,000 pounds (181,437 kilograms)!

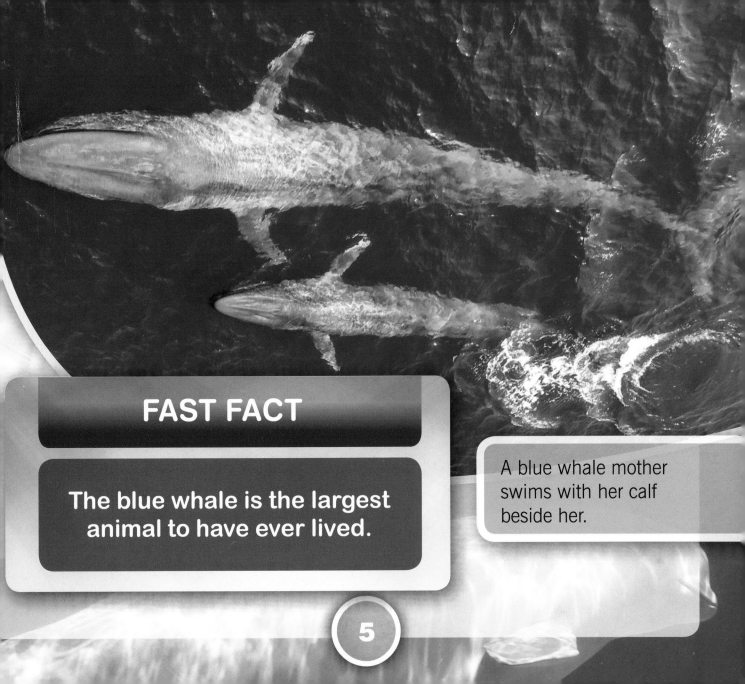

FAST FACT

The blue whale is the largest animal to have ever lived.

A blue whale mother swims with her calf beside her.

PODS

Whales live in oceans all around the world. Some whales feed and travel in groups called pods. Bowhead whale pods may have up to fifty animals!

Beluga whales live in Arctic waters, where it is icy cold.

A pod of beluga whales travel together.

SO MANY KINDS

Scientists say that there are about forty different species of whales. They are sorted into two groups. One group of whales has teeth. The other group does not have teeth.

A gray whale calf shows his baleen.

FAST FACT

Instead of teeth, some whales have a baleen, which helps them catch food.

WHALES ARE MAMMALS

Whales are warm-blooded mammals that breathe air. They rise to the surface and breathe out of one or two blowholes on top of their heads. Then they hold their breath and dive deep.

10

Sperm whales can hold their breath underwater for up to two hours!

A gray whale calf takes in air with its two blowholes.

TIME TO GET MOVING!

Many whales spend parts of the year in cold water near the North or South Pole. They eat and eat and eat! Come spring, they migrate to warmer waters.

FAST FACT

Whales have a layer of fat, called blubber, under their skin to keep them warm in cold waters.

A humpback whale calf jumps out of the freezing water near the North Pole.

13

IN WARMER WATERS

Many mother whales migrate to warmer waters to give birth. A mother whale pushes her calf to the surface for its first breath! Then the calf hungrily drinks its mother's milk.

A newborn sperm whale calf drinks milk from its mother.

UNDERWATER SOUNDS

Clicks, creaks, chirps. Groans, moans, and songs. Whales make many different sounds. Some sounds call for mates. Some sounds help spot food. Some say, "I'm over here, Mom!"

FAST FACT

Beluga whale cows and calves call to each other to stay in contact.

A mother beluga whale and calf stay close together.

17

HUNGRY WHALES

Baleen and toothed whales hunt for food in the ocean. They gobble up fish, squid, and krill. By about six months old, calves are learning how to catch and eat food.

FAST FACT

Sperm whale cows watch each other's calves when they are diving for food.

A Bryde's whale swallows a large group of anchovies.

GUARD THOSE CALVES!

Mother whales keep watch over their calves. Cows guard their calves from **predators**, such as sharks and other whales. Orcas, known as killer whales, may hunt and kill young whales.

A humpback whale guards her calf from danger.

FAST FACT

Humpback whales will protect calves and other marine mammals from orca attacks.

GROWING AND LEARNING

Bowhead calves stay close to their mothers for more than a year. There is much to learn before they are grown up enough to be on their own.

FAST FACT

Scientists figure that bowhead whales can live to be more than two hundred years old.

A bowhead whale must teach her calf how to survive in wild waters.

LEARN MORE

Books

Coleman, Clara. *Whales Work Together.* New York, NY: PowerKids Press, 2017.

Karpik, Joanasie. *Bowhead Whale.* Iqaluit, Nunavut, Canada: Inhabit Media, 2017.

Tunby, Benjamin. *The Whale's Journey.* Minneapolis, MN: Lerner Publications, 2018.

Websites

National Geographic Kids: Blue Whale
kids.nationalgeographic.com/animals/blue-whale/#blue-whale-fluke.jpg
Find out about blue whales.

Whale-World
www.whale-world.com/facts-about-whales-for-kids/
Read fun facts about whales.

INDEX

Published in 2019 by Enslow Publishing, LLC.
101 W. 23rd Street, Suite 240, New York, NY 10011

Copyright © 2019 by Enslow Publishing, LLC.

All rights reserved.

No part of this book may be reproduced by any means without the written permission of the publisher.

Library of Congress Cataloging-in-Publication Data

Names: Idzikowski, Lisa, author.
Title: How whales grow up / Lisa Idzikowski.
Description: New York, NY : Enslow Publishing, 2019. | Series: Animals growing up | Audience: Grades K to 3 | Includes bibliographical references and index. | Identifiers: LCCN 2017049277| ISBN 9780766096639 (library bound) | ISBN 9780766096646 (pbk.) | ISBN 9780766096653 (6 pack)
Subjects: LCSH: Whales—Juvenile literature. | Whales—Infancy—Juvenile literature.
Classification: LCC QL737.C4 I39 2018 | DDC 599.513/92—dc23
LC record available at https://lccn.loc.gov/2017049277

Printed in the United States of America

To Our Readers: We have done our best to make sure all website addresses in this book were active and appropriate when we went to press. However, the author and the publisher have no control over and assume no liability for the material available on those websites or on any websites they may link to. Any comments or suggestions can be sent by email to customerservice@enslow.com.

Photos Credits: Cover, p. 1 Darryl Torckler/The Image Bank/Getty Images; p. 5 Barcroft Media/Getty Images; p. 7 Miles Away Photography/Shutterstock.com; p. 9 Michael Greenfelder/Alamy Stock Photo; p. 11 jo Crebbin/Shutterstock.com; p. 13 Danita Delimont/Gallo Images/Getty Images; p. 15 Fabrice Guerin/Biosphoto/Getty Images; p. 17 CampCrazy Photography/Shutterstock.com; p. 19 kajornyot wildlife photography/Shutterstock.com; p. 21 Yann hubert Shutterstock.com; p. 23 Corey Accardo (NOAA).